The Book Concerning the Tincture of The Philosophers

Unlocking the Secrets of Alchemical Transformation

A Modern Translation

Adapted for the Contemporary Reader

Paracelsus

© Copyright 2025. All rights reserved.

It is not legal to reproduce, duplicate, or transmit any part of this document in either electronic means or in printed format. Recording of this publication is strictly prohibited and any storage of this document is not allowed unless with written permission from the publisher except for the use of brief quotations in a book review.

Table of Contents

Preface - Message to the Reader

Rebuilding the Greatest Library in Human History

Thousands of years ago, the Library of Alexandria was the heart of global knowledge — a sanctuary where the wisdom of every known civilization was gathered and shared freely.

And then, it was lost.

Now, we're rebuilding it — and you are invited to join us.

At the Library of Alexandria, we've set out to make every book available to *every person on Earth* — not just in print, but in every language, every format, and for every reader.

Here's how we do it:

- **Deluxe Print Editions at True Printing Cost** - Order any book as a high-quality paperback, elegant hardcover, or stunning boxset — and only pay what it costs to print. No markups. No middlemen.

- **Unlimited Access to the Greatest Works** - Enjoy thousands of timeless classics — from Plato to Shakespeare to Tolstoy — in beautiful, modern eBook and audiobook editions. Read and listen without limits — for every reader, everywhere.

- **Modern Translations for Every Language & Dialect** - We're reimagining the classics in clear, accessible language — and translating them into every dialect imaginable. Everyone deserves to understand humanity's greatest ideas.

When you visit **LibraryofAlexandria.com**, you're not just accessing books — you're joining a global movement to restore, preserve, and share the wisdom of civilization.

Join us today at LibraryofAlexandria.com

Together, we'll ensure the light of human wisdom never fades again.

With gratitude,
The Modern Library of Alexandria Team

Visit:

www.libraryofalexandria.com

Or scan the code below:

Prologue

Since you, O Sophist, insult me with false and foolish words, saying that, being from rough Helvetia, I am incapable of understanding or learning anything—and also criticize me for being a physician who travels from place to place—I have decided to write this treatise to show the ignorant and inexperienced what true arts existed in the past. I will demonstrate the value of my knowledge against yours, and yours against mine, so that future generations will know how to follow my path in this enlightened age. Look back at Hermes, Archelaus, and others from the early times—see what great philosophers and alchemists lived then. Their work proves that your so-called mentors, O Sophist, are nothing more than empty images and idols. Even if those you call fathers and saints refuse to acknowledge this, the ancient Emerald Tablet reveals more wisdom and skill in philosophy, alchemy, and magic than anything you or your followers could ever teach.

If you still cannot understand how great these treasures are, then tell me: Why did no prince or king ever succeed in conquering the Egyptians? And why did Emperor Diocletian order all the Spagyric books to be burned wherever they could be found? If the contents of those books had remained unknown, the people would have continued to suffer under his oppressive rule. Know this, O Sophist: One day, a yoke just as heavy will be placed upon you and your companions.

In the middle of this age, the authority over all arts has been given to me—Theophrastus Paracelsus, Prince of Philosophy and Medicine. I have been chosen by God to eliminate the empty, false works and misleading words of Aristotle, Galen, Avicenna, Mesva, and their followers. My teachings, which are based on the light of Nature, are solid and unchanging. Though they may seem unappreciated now, in the 1,558th year they will begin to flourish. At that time, people of all kinds—craftsmen and ordinary folk—will see proof through extraordinary signs and fully understand how unshakable the Paracelsian Art is, no matter how hard the sophists try to maintain their flawed knowledge with the support of papal and imperial privileges.

You call me a beggar and wandering sophist, but the Danube and the Rhine rivers will speak in my defense, even if I remain silent. Your lies about me have angered many courts and princes, as well as noble orders and cities. I have a hidden treasure in a city called Weinden, part of Forum Julii, stored at an inn—a treasure so valuable that neither Leo of Rome nor Charles of Germany could buy it, no matter their wealth. Even though the symbol of the star has been applied to your names, only those who follow the divine Spagyric Art know its true meaning.

So, you worm-ridden Sophist, since you think me—a master of hidden knowledge—a foolish and wasteful quack, I now choose to explain, through this treatise, the proper way to prepare and use the famous Tincture of the Philosophers. This explanation is given to honor all who seek the truth and to ensure that those who dismiss the true arts will suffer poverty. This great secret will illuminate the final age, making up for all past losses through divine grace and the reward of true wisdom. From the beginning of the world until now, no growth of knowledge or wisdom will ever have equaled what is to come. In the end, vice will not be able to defeat virtue, and no matter how many resources evil people gather, they will not harm those who remain righteous.

• • •

The Book Concerning The Tincture of The Philosophers

I, Philippus Theophrastus Paracelsus Bombast, declare that, through Divine grace, many different paths have been taken toward discovering the Tincture of the Philosophers. In the end, however, they all reach the same goal. Hermes Trismegistus, the Egyptian, followed his own method. Orus, the Greek, used a similar approach. Hali, the Arabian, stayed committed to his process. Albertus Magnus, the German, also followed a long and complex path. While each of these philosophers advanced according to their chosen methods, they all reached the same outcome—achieving long life, which philosophers have always desired, along with the means to sustain it honorably within this troubled world.

Now, in my time, I, Theophrastus Paracelsus Bombast, Monarch of the Arcana, have been given special gifts by God so that all seekers of this ultimate philosophical knowledge must follow my example. No matter whether they are Italian, Polish, French, or German—or from anywhere else—they must imitate my path. All philosophers, astronomers, and spagyrists, no matter how renowned, must come after me. I will reveal and teach them—both alchemists and doctors—the secrets of bodily regeneration. I will show them the tincture, the hidden knowledge (arcanum), and the quintessence, which contain the foundations of all mysteries and works.

Everyone must only believe in what they have tested through fire, for it is by fire that the truth is separated from falsehood. If someone presents a theory that goes against this method of practical experimentation in alchemy or medicine, there is no reason to trust them. Only those who work in the light of Nature will see this truth, as the light of Nature is given to help us test everything. With this light, we will demonstrate, using the best methods, that those before me—who relied too much on their ideas and speculations—only harmed themselves with their foolishness. For this reason, I have seen many simple people rise to greatness through hard work, while many nobles, trusting only in their imaginations, have fallen into foolishness, thinking of "golden mountains" in their minds before they even touched the fire.

The first things you must learn are digestion, distillation, sublimation, reverberation, extraction, solution, coagulation, fermentation, and fixation. You must also gain experience using all the necessary tools, such as glass vessels, cucurbites, circulators, earthen vessels, baths, blast furnaces, and reverberatory ovens, along with materials like marble, coals, and tongs. Only through mastering these tools and processes will you succeed in alchemy and medicine.

However, as long as you cling to fantasy and opinion, relying on false books, you will never be able to achieve anything in these fields.

• • •

Concerning The Definition of The Subject and Matter of The Tincture of The Philosophers

Before I explain the process of creating the Tincture, it is important to introduce the subject properly. Up until now, this knowledge has been kept hidden by those devoted to truth. The Tincture, when understood in a Spagyric sense, is something that passes from three essences into one through the art of Vulcan—or it can remain in that state. To give it its proper name, as used by the ancients, it is often called the Red Lion, though few truly understand what it is. With the help of Nature and the skill of the alchemist, it can be transformed into a White Eagle, producing two from one. For the alchemist, these two together shine more brightly than gold itself.

If you do not understand the teachings of the Cabalists and the ancient astronomers, then you were neither destined by God for the Spagyric art, nor chosen by Nature for the work of Vulcan, nor created to speak on the subject of alchemy. The essence of the Tincture is a great treasure—like a pearl of immense value—and it is one of the most noble things on earth, second only to the revelation of the Divine and the pursuit of wisdom among men. This Tincture is the true "Lili" of both alchemy and medicine, a treasure that philosophers have sought tirelessly. Yet, because of their incomplete knowledge and lack of proper preparation, they have never achieved the full result. Through their experiments, they managed to discover only the first stage of the Tincture. But the real foundation—the one my fellow alchemists must follow—was left for me to uncover, ensuring that no false ideas would interfere with our true purpose.

With the right to do so, and based on my extensive experience, I correct the errors of other Spagyrists and separate truth from falsehood. Through my long research, I found just reasons to criticize and change many aspects of the old teachings. If I had discovered that the experiments of the ancients were better than my own, I would not have devoted myself to such difficult labor. But I willingly endured these efforts for the benefit and progress of all true alchemists.

Now that I have explained the Tincture and revealed its essence faithfully, in a way that one brother would share with another, I will move on to its preparation. After presenting the discoveries of the earliest ages, I will add my own inventions. In time, the Age of Grace will embrace my contributions, no matter which of the ancient teachers, O Sophist, you choose to follow in the meantime.

• • •

Concerning The Process of The An- Cients For The Tincture of The Philo- Sophers, and a More Compendious Method

The old Spagyrists left Lili to decay for a philosophical month, after which they distilled the liquid spirits from it until the dry spirits rose to the surface. They then soaked the leftover matter, known as *caput mortuum*, with the liquid spirits again and continued to extract the spirits through repeated distillation, until all the dry spirits were elevated. After this, they combined the extracted moisture and dry spirits in a pelican flask, repeating this three or four times, until the entire substance of Lili became dry and settled at the bottom.

Although early experiments provided this process before full fixation, the ancient alchemists still often achieved their goal using this method. However, they could have reached the treasure of the Red Lion much faster if they had understood the connection between astronomy and alchemy, as I have revealed in the *Apocalypse of Hermes*. Yet, as Christ said to comfort the faithful, "Each day has enough trouble of its own." For the Spagyrists who came before my time, the work was long and difficult. But now, with the help of the Holy Spirit guiding us, my theory and practice will make the process easier and clearer for those who persevere with patience.

Through my experiments, I have come to understand the properties of Nature—its essences, processes, and transformations—which are the highest gifts a philosopher can receive. These truths have remained hidden from the sophists until now. In ancient times, the first experiments with the Tincture led the Spagyrists to divide one thing into two. When this knowledge was later lost in the Middle Ages, those who followed searched diligently and rediscovered the two aspects of this one thing. They named it Lili, recognizing it as the essence needed for the Tincture.

These alchemists, imitating the processes of Nature, allowed the substance to decay like a seed planted in the ground. For, just as a seed must rot before it can grow, the hidden power of the Tincture could only emerge after the matter had undergone this corruption. They first extracted the liquid spirits, then, with the intense heat of fire, raised the dry spirits in the same way. The process followed Nature's rhythm, with each stage maturing in its own time, like the farmer harvesting crops when the seasons change.

Finally, just as summer follows spring, they brought together the fruits and dry spirits, completing the Mastery of the Tincture. At last, it reached the stage of ripening, ready to be harvested.

. . .

Concerning The Process for The Tincture of The Philosophers, As It Is Shortened

The ancient Spagyrists would not have needed such long, tiring work if they had studied under my teachings. They could have achieved the same results with far less effort and cost. But now that I, Theophrastus Paracelsus, the Monarch of Arcana, have arrived, the time has come to uncover what was hidden from all Spagyrists before me. So, I say this: Take only the rose-colored blood from the Lion and the glue from the Eagle. Mix them together and follow the old process to solidify them, and you will have the Tincture of the Philosophers—a treasure sought by many but found by few.

Whether you like it or not, Sophist, this work exists within Nature itself. It is a marvelous gift from God that surpasses the natural world and is one of the most precious treasures in this world of suffering. At first glance, it might seem insignificant that one substance can be changed into something far nobler than it originally was. But you must admit that this transformation is a miracle created by the Spagyrist, who, through his preparations, breaks down a lowly substance to awaken a new, more valuable essence. If you have learned anything from Aristotle's wisdom, or from us, or from the teachings of Serapio, then show it through experiment. Maintain the dignity of scholarship, as a true lover of knowledge and a doctor should. But if you know nothing and can achieve nothing, why do you treat me with such scorn, as if I were an ignorant cow from Helvetia, and insult me as a mere wanderer?

Art is a second Nature—a complete world of its own, as proven through experience, which stands against you and your idols. Alchemists often combine different simple substances, which they then transform as needed to create something new. Out of many things, they can form one, producing effects that go beyond what Nature alone can achieve. For example, in Gastaynum, it is well known that Venus is made from Saturn; in Carinthia, Luna is created from Venus; and in Hungary, Sol is produced from

Luna. There are many other natural transformations known to the Magi, more astonishing than anything told in Ovid's *Metamorphoses*.

To understand me fully, search for your Lion in the East and your Eagle in the South for the work at hand. You will not find better tools than those produced in Hungary and Istria. If you wish to work with the concept of unity through duality in trinity, then journey southward. In Cyprus, you will find what you seek. However, I must not reveal more on this topic here. There are many more hidden secrets involving transformations, though few know of them. Even though God may reveal these secrets to anyone, the knowledge of this Art does not spread widely, for the Almighty grants understanding only to those who know how to conceal such wisdom until the time of Elias the Artist, when nothing hidden will remain undiscovered.

You can also see with your own eyes—though I need not say it, for some might mock—that within the fire of Sulfur lies a great tincture for gems, one that elevates them beyond what Nature alone can achieve. But I will not discuss the process of refining metals and gems here, as I have already written enough on the subject in my *Secret of Secrets*, my book on the *Vexations of Alchemists*, and other works. Having begun with the process used by our ancestors in making the Tincture of the Philosophers, I will now complete it fully.

• • •

The End

Thank you for Reading

You've Just Read a Piece of the Greatest Library Ever Rebuilt

Thank you for reading.

This book is one of thousands we're restoring, reimagining, and translating as part of the **Modern Library of Alexandria** — a global movement to preserve and share humanity's most important ideas.

What was once lost to fire and time is now rising again — not just as memory, but as living, breathing knowledge, freely accessible to all.

What You Can Do Next:

- **Keep Reading.**

  Discover more legendary works — in beautiful print, audiobook, or digital form — at LibraryofAlexandria.com.

- **Build Your Own Library.**

  Every title is available as a paperback, hardcover, or collectible boxset — at true printing cost. Craft a personal library worthy of display.

- **Spread the Light.**

  Share this book. Tell others about the movement. Help us translate every timeless work into every language, so no reader is ever left behind.

By finishing this book, you've already taken part in something extraordinary.

Join us at LibraryofAlexandria.com

Together, we're rebuilding the greatest library the world has ever known.

With appreciation,
The Modern Library of Alexandria Team

Visit:

www.libraryofalexandria.com

Or scan the code below: